Hello Spring
TO:
FROM:

The blooming spring is the
smile of the ever-joyful nature.
~ James Herriot

April is the kindest month. April gets you out of your head and out working in the garden

Marty Rubin

You are
reborn with
the roses, in
every spring

Juan Ramón Jiménez

A perfect spring day! Enjoy it while it lasts because you don't know what's coming

Marty Rubin

Spring is painted in daffodil yellows, robin egg blues, new grass green and the brightness of hope for a better life

Spring will come and so will happiness. Hold on. Life will get warmer

Mary Bly

The promise of spring's arrival is enough to get anyone through the bitter winter!

Jen Selinsky

You can cut all the flowers but you cannot keep spring from coming

Pablo Neruda

Spring is the fountain of love for thirsty winter

MUNIA KHAN

THE FIRST
BLOOMS OF SPRING
ALWAYS MAKE MY
HEART SING

S. Brown

SPRING IS THE TIME OF THE YEAR WHEN IT IS SUMMER IN THE SUN AND WINTER IN THE SHADE

Nan Porter

The point is that
the pleasures of
spring are available
to everybody, and
cost nothing

George Orwell

Despite the heart numbing frost, my soul is blooming like spring

Debasish Mridha

Spring is the time of plans and projects

Leo Tolstoy

SPRING IS NATURE'S
WAY OF SAYING,
"LET'S PARTY!

ROBIN WILLIAMS

SPRING IS NOT A SEASON;
IT IS A MYSTERIOUS
ILLUSIONIST WHO SETS
OFF FIREWORKS IN THE
DEPTHS OF OUR SOUL!

MEHMET MURAT ILDAN

Spring is a season of the soul to regain its strength

Lailah Gifty Akita

Spring shows what God can do with a drab and dirty world

Virgil A. Kraft

I love the
smell of rain
and growing
things

Alexis Flora Hope